Jesse James Wroblewski

—

MARKETING

FOR

SUPERVILLAINS

VOLUME 2

An Academic Framework To Achieve Your
Unfair Marketing Advantage

ISBN: Hardcover 979-8-9890673-3-6
ISBN: Paperback 979-8-9890673-4-3
ISBN: Ebook 979-8-9890673-5-0

Design and publishing assistance by The Happy Self-Publisher.

DEDICATION

To the villains of today, who are the visionaries of tomorrow.

TABLE OF CONTENTS

INTRODUCTION

"Who are you to be anonymous?
You, whose name should be spoken in reverent tones or
in terrified whispers?
Who are you to deny greatness?
If you deny yourself, you deny the entire world, and we
will not be denied.
Greatness awaits!"

— *Snippet of a monologue from PlayStation*
New Zealand "Greatness Awaits" Commercial

Who are you to be forgotten?
You're someone's "best-kept secret," always there to answer the call, yet you remain just that, a secret, a legend, only known to few.

You, who have accomplished the impossible, who have bent reality to your will, who have achieved feats that should echo through the halls of history - yet your name remains unspoken, your legacy untold.

This is the greatest crime of all: the crime of anonymity.

Consider this: a hulking monster named Doomsday, the being who achieved what legions of villains could only dream of - he killed Superman. Let that sink in. He accomplished what Lex Luthor, Brainiac, and countless others failed to do. He defeated the Man of Steel himself.

Yet, ask any person on the street to name Superman's greatest enemy, and they'll stammer out "Lex Luthor" while Doomsday's name fades into obscurity. Why? Because Doomsday was all substance, no style. All achievements, no advertisement. A cautionary tale of power without propaganda. All steak, no sizzle.

But perhaps you think this fate only befalls fictional figures? Then heed the tale of Otto Frederick Rohwedder, the man who revolutionized human civilization with the greatest invention since... well, since his own invention: Sliced bread. For ten years - TEN YEARS - his miraculous machine gathered dust while humanity continued the barbaric practice of manually carving their loaves like savages. A decade of potential greatness was squandered because he failed to properly market his masterpiece and ultimately sold the rights to the Micro-Westco Co. of Bettendorf, Iowa.

No, achieving great things is no longer enough; being your clients' best-kept secret is a fool's errand. Unless that client provides enough of an incentive to remain behind the scenes (i.e., they pay you dearly to remain their best-kept secret.)

Who are you to deny your greatness? If you deny yourself, you deny the entire world. Your achievements, your innovations, your conquests - they deserve more than to be footnotes in history. They deserve billboards and headlines, viral videos, and trending topics. It makes no difference whether your personal preference is that your name be spoken in reverent tones or in terrified whispers. *It must be spoken.*

This book isn't about teaching you to be great. You're already great. This is about ensuring the world knows it, fears it, celebrates it. Because greatness without marketing isn't greatness at all - it's a tragedy.

Greatness awaits. But more importantly, greatness demands to be noticed.

Welcome to Marketing for Supervillains...Volume 2.

CHAPTER 1

THE WHYS & THE HOWS

> *"To confront a villain, you must understand him.*
> *And once you understand him...*
> *You may become him."*
>
> **— Custom MSV Doctrine, Article I**

Who would ever want **MORE** supervillains in the world? Me.

And on your quest of reading this tome to its completion, you will no doubt waver on agreeing with me, but I assure you, ultimately, you will feel the desire for more supervillains as well because, after all, you and I... we're not so different.

I began MSV Volume 1 with my best take on the all-too-common supervillain trope "We're Not So Different, You And I." You can see this scenario play out in countless hero/villain face-offs from the more recent movies like *Fast & The Furious 4*, *Raiders Of The Lost Ark*, *Harry Potter and The Deathly Hallows* and iconically spouted by Willem Dafoe as the Green Goblin in *Spider-man*.

This trope is not isolated to instances where Hollywood writers get lazy and need something for the villain to say when he has his prey right where he wants them. No, this sentiment can be traced as far back as William Shakespeare's *The Merchant of Venice*. The main character, a Jew named Shylock, faces his Christian assailants who are hell-bent on revenge, and asks, "If you prick us (Jews) do we not bleed?" Are we so different?

We can see how all too familiar this line has become when it was perfectly parodied by Dr. Evil, practically rolling his eyes at his captor in *Austin Powers in Goldmember*. An event so common it would seem odd NOT to poke fun at the scene in a movie that specifically lampoons such scenarios.

WHY?

You may be asking yourself why; why did I start my first book, focused on differentiation, with a statement that is so commonplace? (The book is now available on Amazon and everywhere books are sold. Yes, a shameless marketing plug, but I will not remain anonymous.)

More importantly, why is this sentiment so prevalent in media throughout human history? There must be something hidden in those words; a 4D chess maneuver that most common observers simply overlook.

Once we learn that, we'll uncover the **HOW.** How do we, marketing supervillains, utilize this statement and the strategy behind it to further our own lofty aspirations?

It was in this spirit that MSV Volume 2 was created.

MSV Volume 1 is not required reading to appreciate everything in Volume 2. You, by picking up this book, however, have declared yourself as someone who is clearly committed to achieving greatness and deserves to have Volume 1 in your hallowed library.

Might I suggest the hardcover? You deserve it.

For now, allow me to take you under my wing and foster your questions about the actual how-to process of becoming a Marketing Supervillain. Why would I do this? Because, as you asked at the beginning of this very chapter... Who would ever want **MORE** supervillains in the world... I do.

Now let's get to work!

CHAPTER 2

WE ARE NOT MONSTERS

"See, I'm not a monster... I'm just ahead of the curve."
— the Joker, The Dark Knight

Seasoned marketers like us have walked different, unique paths in life. Through these paths, we have been subjected to countless designs that have been kneecapped by bad decisions of the ignorant, as well as brilliant marketing suggestions and strategies hobbled by the short-sighted. We have, metaphorically, like the Joker, crawled through the seedy underbelly of the crime-infested slums of Gotham City.

Do you know, according to the Joker, what separates him from the rest of us?

ONE BAD DAY.

One bad day is all it takes to birth your inner supervillain. The Joker was once a regular guy, a stand-up comedian with a loving wife and a baby on the way, until one day, one *bad* day, his world was turned upside down when all was taken from him.

This one bad day changed the trajectory of the Joker's life and made him what he is today.

One. Bad. Day.

Great supervillains know themselves, and even more so, they know the world they are trying to conquer. And as such, they engage in a piece of the Socratic Method called Aporia.

Aporia is the method, most often practiced in debates, where the speaker attempts to create a window of doubt in the mind of someone whose mind appears to be made up on an issue. They hope to make them realize that they were not as set in their thinking as they had once thought.

No more perfect example of aporia exists than the Joker's eloquent declaration to Batman, "To them, you're just a freak… like me."

The Joker does not care about the usual things supervillains care about: money, fame, power. To quote him exactly, *"This town deserves a better class of criminal and I'm going to give it to them."*

The Joker's sole goal, his crowning achievement, would be to show the world that the incorruptible is indeed able to be corrupted.

The symbol of this incorruptibility is the Batman. Batman stands for all that is lawful and just in society.

The Joker's grand plan is to show the world that even the righteous Batman can be corrupted. The Joker is so obsessed with his mission that he has no problem going to extremes to show that Batman is able to be pushed over the guardrails of his own mission statement, "No killing." The Joker's commitment is so strong that, to prove his point, he is willing to lose his life to Batman.

He tells Batman of how the law itself, the police, with whom Bats has an uneasy alliance, would simply throw him (Batman) away the moment anything went awry. Deep down, as much as

Batman wants to be known as a symbol of justice, he knows the Joker's statement is true.

"To them," he says, "you're just a freak... like me."

YOU AND I... WE'RE NOT SO DIFFERENT

For us marketers, maybe it was one bad day... or perhaps, it was an accumulation of a smaller bad minutes over the course of a career.

The Joker has experienced the absolute worst the world could throw at him, and in our world, the marketing world, the tragedies and bad decisions we've had to endure have only tempered our resolve. We've gone through the looking glass and come out the other side enlightened with a different view of the marketplace. Our clients, on the other hand, are still on the other side of the glass, seemingly fighting us at every turn.

The Joker is not afraid to acknowledge that while everyone claims to be civilized and have high morals, moral turpitude lurks beneath the surface. As he puts it: "When the chips are down, these civilized people... they'll eat each other. See, I'm not a monster... I'm just ahead of the curve."

As Marketing Supervillains with an advanced, evolved perspective, we, too, are ahead of the curve. A client with a rosy, optimistic fix-all suggestion, such as starting a social media account to boost sales, may seem as laughable to an MSV as a Gotham City citizen telling Batman or the Joker to let the police do their job and wait for due process.

No, for better or worse, we experienced and hardened marketing professionals have seen how deep the rabbit hole is. Our one bad day is behind us, our origin story has been written. We can no longer remain silent and assume the roles of order takers; we will demand to be noticed and possibly feared.

CHAPTER 3

MY ONE BAD DAY

"The system isn't broken. It was built this way."

— Custom MSV Doctrine, Article ZERO

April 19, 2019 ... MSV Jesse James Wroblewski's **ONE BAD DAY** The crazy client.

You may be thinking, of course, we're not so different, we all have crazy client stories. You may be thinking that you, in fact, have the craziest client of them all, but allow me to challenge that notion.

Leading up to this bad day, there had been little things that began to chip away at me. I'm sure they are not so different from the challenges you too face as professional marketers.

In my earlier days as a marketer, I felt like Batman. Each night, I would come home to the little red blinking light on my answering machine illuminating my mom's basement, like the Bat-Signal lighting the sky of Gotham City. My special skills were needed.

Just a few years later. I'd step into my office and see that same blinking light, and I would be filled with horror, I went from puffing out my chest in excitement to sulking in existential dread.

Not another voicemail from these damn needy citizens.

Little by little, my clients would chip away at my designs and masterfully crafted campaigns, and thus, ultimately, as I interpreted it, at me. But I pushed forward because you make hay when the sun shines.

I hired a crew of minions and rented an office.

Now, in addition to my internal drive to do meaningful work and my primal drive to not starve, I also had to make sure the rent was paid and my minions ate as well.

And then it happened, my ONE BAD DAY:

Payroll was right around the corner.

A prospect came in with an open checkbook, literally.

He wanted to pay us for discovery.

The first red flag was that he insisted on paying in multiples of 11. Meaning every check he wrote to our organization was something to satisfy his numerology fetish, literally writing out checks in the amount of $1,111.11, $2,222.22, and $5,555.55. My bookkeeper hated me ... and him.

The second red flag was that he insisted every individual in my organization sign an NDA before we could hear his master plan. He also insisted on giving each person a payment in exchange for their NDA. Wanna guess the amount, my MSV-in-training? Yep ... $111.11. I wasn't sure if that was even legal, but that soon became the least of my concerns because the real shit show began.

If you've had your personal fill of insanity from the weird parallel universe where crazy clients seem to populate, I'll spare you the details of the meeting. But for those with a sick, voyeuristic itch that has to be scratched, I've uploaded the actual live footage from the interaction onto my YouTube page via a private link here: https://bit.ly/4mfHtgG.

In short, within the hallowed halls of my office, there were masks worn, a stuffed goose presented, and golden eggs offered, all without the utterance of a single word. And no, I am not speaking metaphorically. At first, I found the whole situation intriguing and funny, and, well, that financial bump to the corporate bank account was a welcome addition.

But as I looked around at the blank stares on the confused and annoyed faces of my crew, I realized the gravity of the situation - I had become my own worst nightmare, I had become a sellout.

We were prostituting our talents to the highest bidder in a landscape of unappreciative clients.

I knew it was time for a drastic change. But what and how?

How do I attract only meaningful work but continue to put food on the table for me and my loyal team?

CHAPTER 4

SCREW IT!

> *"Everyone wants to be better, but no one wants to change"*
>
> **—unknown**

It was time to figure out this mess. I was doing what seemed absolutely natural for me to utilize the outer limits of my creativity so my clients could shine in a crowded marketplace, and I was good at it!

But like some cosmic joke, I learned about something else that was absolutely natural: a cognitive bias called loss aversion.

Humans have a primal need for safety and security. The psychological pain of losing something feels twice as powerful as the pleasure of gaining something.

The late Nobel Prize-winning economist, Daniel Kahneman, suggested that if you offered a group of people an investment opportunity with an 80% chance of success, most people would enthusiastically take that chance.

Yet, if you proposed an investment opportunity to that same group of people but instead reframed it as having a 20% chance of failure, those very same people would decline the opportunity, even though that proposal is just the other side of the same coin.

While my clients came to me proudly displaying the top 10% of their iceberg [to push the limits of their marketing, for me to tap deeply into my most creative concepts], they were unconsciously motivated by the bottom 90%, which was fear of change. Their directive was not in alignment with their desires, and the overall effect is that this dichotomy unconditionally destroys our ability as creatives to act in the best interest of our clients' business growth.

A pretty damn funny joke from the universe.

My one superpower of using my creativity to make my clients stand out goes against everything humans are programmed to think.

Back to the drawing board.

My ego screamed SCREW IT! I thought, what if I become WORLD CLASS at what I do—made my projects so damn good no one could possibly reject them? What if I did better than my absolute best?

My mind jumped from one possibility to the next:

- I'll learn new skills! I'll offer more to my clients, things they can't get anywhere else!
- I'll refine my existing skill set. I'll take that expensive course that gives me a certificate for my wall.
- I'll wait until I inevitably sign that prestigious client who will whisk me away to the land of exclusive and elusive prospects.

I sat and schemed, feeling like Jack Nicholson, smugly thinking, "Wait 'til they get a load of me!"

Maybe you have had these thoughts as well?

Then, I learned a demoralizing story.

Steve Jobs.

A marketing genius. A visionary. A man who created what is widely considered the greatest television commercial of all time, the infamous 1984 Macintosh ad. A dystopian, Orwellian masterpiece featuring a lone, defiant heroine hurling a sledgehammer through the screen of a droning dictator, symbolizing Apple's promise to shatter the conformity of IBM's stranglehold on the PC market. As the screen fades to black, the voiceover delivers the chilling tagline:

"You'll see why 1984 won't be like 1984."

Perfection. A masterstroke. The pinnacle of what advertising could be.

And guess what happened?

Apple's board of directors got cold feet. They pulled the plug.

If Jobs hadn't had the conviction and the capital to air the ad himself, we might have never seen it. The greatest commercial of all time nearly lost to a room of non-creatives and bean counters.

That's when it hit me. If Steve Jobs (STEVE FREAKIN' JOBS!) had to fight tooth and nail against corporate fear and mediocrity (safety?) just to get his masterpiece out into the world, what hope did I have?

I had spent my career thinking I was the only creative visionary forced to double as a part-time therapist for my clients and a full-time psychological chess player, constantly strategizing how to push bold ideas past the committee of the clueless. But no. This wasn't unique to me. This was the Kobayashi Maru, the infamous no-win scenario from MSV Volume 1.

Much like Captain Kirk, the only man who was inventive enough to realize the only way to beat the Kobayashi Maru was to rewrite the rules, I too realized I had to do the same. If the game were rigged, I wouldn't play it. I'd change it.

I had to rewrite the rules of the game to ensure that I won the battle Every. Single. Time.

PART 1

THE 6-STEP PLAN TO BECOMING AN MSV

CHAPTER 5

THE MISSION STEPS

"I used to think I was the hero. Turns out, I was just the last one to realize I'd been played."

— MSV Doctrine Article VI

Since you and I are not so different, this battle is not just mine, it's yours too.

Since you and I are not so different, you too are not here to play by the rules.

Since you and I are not so different, you've experienced the same frustration. You've seen brilliant, bright ideas reduced to a dull beige. You've faked smiles while your concepts were gutted by some weak, fear-driven committee.

So here's your wake-up call: it's time to weaponize everything they tried to suppress in you. It's time to flip the script.

I've concocted a precise, six-step plan, meticulously engineered to awaken the dark genius within you. This is not some feel-good fluff or watered-down "how-to" for beige-brand do-gooders. This is the blueprint for you to ignite chaos, disrupt mediocrity, and *own* the game.

Each step is a rung on the ladder that descends into the underworld of marketing mayhem:

The Realization

This is your sacred spark. The moment your third eye pries itself open and beholds the twisted "reality" that surrounds you. The clients, the committees, the endless cycles of "play it safe", the drivel that guts your genius, suddenly it all clicks. The veil lifts, and you realize: this world wasn't built *for you*. It was built to *contain you*. This is your point of no return, where conformity dies and your villainous vision is born in a blaze of righteous rebellion.

The One Thing

This is your Holy Grail, your unforgiving Why, your core of unshakable power. It's not just a differentiator, it's your identity. The One Thing is your uncut essence, the raw core of your power, the thing that, once you find it, makes your competition irrelevant. Forget generic USPs or elevator pitches. This is your Excalibur, forged in fire and sharpened by every rejection you've ever endured. With it, you don't compete. You dominate.

The Exclamation

Enough whispering in the shadows. The Exclamation is your full-throated roar, your "Kali Ma!" moment, your declaration of marketing war. It's not just an announcement, it's a detonation. Your war cry. Your declaration to the world that everything's about to change. The world will know your name, not because you politely introduced yourself, but because you kicked in the damn doors and declared, "I'm not here to play. I'm here to win."

The Madness

This isn't a tactic, it's your glorious, unhinged masterpiece. Identifying and leaning into the Madness is your plan, your method to the mayhem. It's the precise sequence of chaos you've engineered to blow minds and rewrite rules. The Madness is brilliance dressed as insanity, clever enough to work and nuts enough to be unforgettable.

The Sacrifice

Every metamorphosis demands a price. Blood, sleep, ego - something's gotta go. This is where you break the chains of mediocrity by paying the toll in time, tears, or even, perhaps, tarnished relationships. It hurts, as it should. Because comfort is the enemy of transformation. You don't rise without something burning. The Sacrifice is your scorched-earth vow to never go back, no matter what it costs.

The Aftermath

When the smoke clears and the dust settles, they'll speak of you in hushed tones. Some will curse your name. Others will carve it into the walls of the industry. The Aftermath is not just su rvival, it's your coronation. You didn't just weather the storm. You became the storm. Your legend will outlive the fads, the algorithms, and the beige brand noise. This is your empire, born in villainy, hardened through adversity.

This isn't a journey. It's an *origin story*.

Now sharpen your claws and prepare to take what is rightfully yours.

Let the villainy begin.

CHAPTER 6

STEP 1: THE REALIZATION

"They fear you. They should."

— Magneto

Exploding scoreboards, on-field TNT detonations, riots, and even... (gasp) mimes! These may all sound like preludes to a disaster, but they were all tactics of a multi-generational family of Marketing Supervillains.

Let's start at the most famous, or infamous, in this case.

The Date: July 12, 1979
The Place: Chicago, IL
The Venue: Comiskey Park
The Event: Disco Demolition Night

After a tepid reception for disco appreciation night at the ballpark, Mike Veeck, in an effort to give the disco haters a night to remember, decided to tap into the complete opposite demographic. Mike was the marketing director for the Chicago White Sox, whose sole responsibility was to fill the 35,000-seat stadium, which rarely surpassed 2/3 occupancy.

So he decided to run a promotion that offered 99-cent tickets to every fan who entered the stadium and brought with them a disco album that would be blown up on the field. How do you blow up an expected 20,000+ disco albums? In a dumpster full of dynamite between games of a doubleheader, of course!

Well, Mike and his security staff had severely underestimated the dislike of disco and/or the love of 99-cent tickets, because the normally 66% full stadium was overfilled to capacity... 250% over! 90,000 people showed up to participate in the event. While Mike underestimated the response to his offer, he also overestimated the quantity of explosives needed to complete the task.

A stadium overpacked with rowdy and rambunctious disco-hating acolytes, combined with the steaming black crater where centerfield once resided, resulted in the White Sox forfeiting the second game of the doubleheader.

Sure, one perspective was that of a disaster, but Mike did his job as a marketing supervillain to a tee. You see, Mike and his father, Bill Veeck, then owner of the Chicago White Sox, not only became notorious for their outrageous marketing stunts, but also firmly built their business on them.

Bill Veeck gained notoriety by installing the world's first (and only) exploding scoreboard, which would set off a glorious fireworks display every time the White Sox hit a home run. He would employ circus acts to make slow points in the game more engaging. Outside of the stadium, clowns, jugglers, and, yes, even mimes would entice fans to purchase tickets, lest they be left out of what happened at the park, which wasn't typically shown on television.

Just the title of Mike's book, *Another Boring, Derivative, Piece of Crap Business Book*, guarantees him a future spot in the YouTube Marketing Supervillain Hall Of Fame (yes, it does exist.)

Mike's marketing acumen didn't just stop at bringing patrons into ballparks. Armed with the knowledge that 75% of people who purchase a business book only read the first chapter, Mike decided to cram the entire book into Chapter 1 so everyone would read it to the end. How's that for a Kobyashi Maru?

Deep inside that chapter is a statistic that cleared up a lot of confusion for me.

Research shows that 85% of people will, on-site, outrightly reject a new idea. The reasons for the rejection are as follows:

- 35% "It's Not My Idea"
- 25% "Too Many Things Wrong With It"
- 25% "This Will Upset My Routine"

So think about that.

Our role as marketers, similar to supervillains, is that we are agents of change. We are most often contacted when the proverbial defecation is about to hit the rotating oscillator. We are reached out to, not when everything is going hunky-dory, but when some underling in the broken marketing department of the company is about to lose their job. Their pain is great, and we are both the anesthesia and the antidote.

We are not hired to toe the company line and maintain the status quo of their marketing. We are, 99% of the time, hired to usher in new ideas.

Time and time again, our creativity is called upon to create change.

We swoop in ready to take our role as the hero. We bring groundbreaking, problem-solving ideas, BUT since 85% of the population of planet Earth is predisposed to reject change, our ideas get hobbled and, by association, we can feel rejected as well.

At this point, you probably feel like an outcast. Congratulations.

I call this step **THE REALIZATION**, the first step in becoming an MSV.

The realization is that you, a marketing professional, are an agent of change.

This realization should be a shift in mindset; you should no longer see yourself as the superhero, swooping in to save the day with your creative ideas. No, instead, you rush in, forcing people to change their patterns of behavior or their perception of what their brand really is. No matter how great your idea is, you will likely be met with strong opposition.

The sooner you recognize and accept that, the quicker you can, like Mike and his father, begin to change the rules of the game.

Welcome to the club. You're in good company.

CHAPTER 7

STEP 2: THE ONE THING

"*Differentiation isn't a tactic. It's a declaration of war against being ignored.*"

— MSV Doctrine, Article VII

Now that we have identified the **realization** of your place as a Marketing Supervillain, you need your Hyperborean Particle Blaster, because every Marketing Supervillain worth their weight has a Hyperborean Particle Blaster. You do have one, don't you? Oh wait...

Commoners know it as a freeze ray. (But you're not a commoner, you have realized you *are* a Marketing Supervillain or, at the very least, an MSV in the making.)

And as I'm sure you all know, the crucial ingredient for a freeze ray is...????

Helium-Based Plasma. (Give yourself 20 Supervillain points if you knew the answer to that question.)

So you go online and search for Helium-Based Plasma, and you can't decide which to buy.... They all look the same because the Helium-Based Plasma market has become... commoditized.

So, how will you decide which ammunition to purchase for your freeze ray? It's likely that will be determined by price.

Now, if your clients are as uneducated on marketing as you are on Helium-Based Plasma, how will they choose who to work with?

You'd like to think they could appreciate the quality of your portfolio. But what do they know? They couldn't tell a Rembrandt from rest-stop toilet stall graffiti.

You'd like to think they know the importance of pixel-perfect design or W3 compliance.

You'd love to believe those highly educated clients who appreciate your refined skill sets are out there...

I personally got tired of searching for them. So the question becomes:

How do you make sure your clients never look at you the way we look at commoditized Helium-Based Plasma?

Or in simpler terms... **HOW DO WE BECOME... DECOMMODITIZED?**

This question has fascinated, (perhaps even haunted) me for the longest time.

After Microsoft Word had continuously corrected me, claiming "decommoditized" wasn't a word, I realized I must have created it, and did what any self-respecting supervillain would do: I trademarked Decommoditized™. (Just looking at that little raised TM brings a tear of pride to my eye.)

I became fascinated with the question and passionate about finding answers because, after much denial, I realized, my MSV, I had become the dreaded C-word: commoditized.

This brings us to Step #2 in the process of birthing your Marketing Supervillain: **THE ONE THING.**

Many business books will tell you to find your differentiator, which in some cases is interchangeably used as your Unique Selling Proposition (USP), which, as any good MSV would know...

is B.S. Well, at least it's not 100% accurate.

Uncovering your meaningful differentiator is your brand's mic-drop moment. While USP's can be easily stolen or co-opted (we're the purest - the cheapest, the most accessible water,) your meaningful differentiator is like a fi ngerprint, impossible to replicate without a soul transplant. Could you imagine someone trying to copy Liquid Death's rebellion-in-a-can differentiation? It'd be an obvious, cheap parody.

The acronym creators of the world leave out the monumental task of discovering your "ONE thing," your singular differentiator, your one planet from the universe of differentiation, **THE ONE THING** that makes you stand out in a commoditized marketplace. The Universe of Differentiation is how I co dified my pro cess of uncovering meaningful differentiation for your brand.

Second, they leave out how you are going to convey your one special thing to the world.

In Volume 1 (conveniently made available for e-readers MSV's on the go!), I delved deep into the Universe of Differentiation. I codified how brands throughout history, both large and small, have successfully decommoditized themselves using one (or more) of the planets in this universe.

I've made this guide readily available for all aspiring MSVs at www.decommoditized.com as a 1-page document, complete with a "secret decoder" key to get you started.

These 12 planets and the examples provided in the book are your guide to identifying at least one authentic differentiator that will become your North Star (pun intended).

When people hear the word differentiated or different, it's often interpreted with a negative connotation.

Often, it is interpreted as meaning odd or weird.

Typically, I get asked, "Do I need to be outlandish to become differentiated?" and the answer is absolutely not.

Brands like Tiffany, Sotheby's, and Steinway are all included within the universe of differentiation.

The process of finding your ONE thing covers key differentiation tactics on everything from G.I. Joe to Rolex watches.

Is the process challenging?

Yes.

Is it rewarding? Absolutely.

And when have any MSVs ever backed down from a challenge?

Remember, when uncovering your ONE thing, specificity creates credibility, and credibility leads to clients placing more trust in your expertise. Once you apply this to YOUR brand, THEN you can begin leveraging the universe for your clients' brands as well.

This ONE thing (your true, meaningful differentiator) will allow you to rewrite all the rules of how the game is played.

CHAPTER 8

STEP #3 THE EXCLAMATION

"Every great idea begins as blasphemy to the unimaginative."

— Marketing Supervillain Doctrine, Section 1.1

I have a little confession to make. In my browser, I have a folder decided that to contains go in another links to direction. all of the Perhaps clients I'm who petty, told but me maybe, they, just maybe, you and I are not so different.

Every few months, when I'm bored, I check in on these clients and almost always find out that the "other direction" they decided to go in was clearly the wrong one. The website or brand they finally wound up choosing was, in my opinion, the wrong one, especially when compared to the magic I would have brought forth into the world on their behalf. But sure enough, in due time, that crappy website, shortly after launch, would wind up going through a redesign, or, in some cases, lead to a 404 error because they went out of business.

I always waited, rather impatiently, I must admit, for them to come crawling back, but they rarely ever did. In my head, I figured they had tried all the rest, now they'll humble themselves and come crawling back to me and my firm - clearly in my mind, the best - but they rarely did.

The simple fact is, I wanted them to Rue The Day they had ever decided to travel on their business journey without this MSV leading the charge!

You may think this sounds overly dramatic, but it's a sentiment so entwined in our DNA that it needs to be acknowledged even if it's not smiled upon in the ever-strengthening "Positive Vibes Only" crowd across social media.

Mark my words... I'll make them RUE THE DAY!

The word "rue" comes from the Old English **"hrēowan,"** which means "to make sorry" or "to cause to feel regret." This statement or feeling is so primal that the earliest recorded instance of it was in the early 17th century by the infamous William Shakespeare. He used this famous line in Othello.

"O, thou wilt rue this time" (Act 5, Scene 2)

Rue The Day is a pivotal statement exclaimed by an average citizen when they have finally hit their tipping point. For the average citizen, it is simply an empty promise. For you, my new MSV friend, it is the first birthing contraction of your inner supervillain.

THIS TOWN WILL RUE THE DAY IT EVER CROSSED ME!

This is a sentiment so primal that it lies buried beneath the thin veil of civility, rarely summoned but devastating when unleashed. Let's not just harness it... let's *weaponize* it.

Sometimes anger and frustration are your best motivators, and they need to be acknowledged and, more importantly, utilized as the motivational force for which they were intended in our DNA.

When someone makes a "You'll rue the day!" exclamation, they most often use it to release the steam from their emotional pressure cooker. That is not why this or any such statement has been created. It's been created to be your catalyst, your motivator to change both you and your F'n industry! Use it for its intended purpose.

What do you stand for in your industry? It's not an easy question to answer... until you tap into Rue The Day.

Create a list of everything you perceive as wrong in your industry, every mistake a client has made, every screw-up a competitor is chasing. It's okay if you feel like you are whining. Every now and then, a good whine can be valuable in creating the momentum to change. Often, whining, a really good, gut-wrenching *"this F'N industry of mine!"* leads to a much-needed epiphany. So, whine away, my MSV friend. But, I caution you, don't let the whining release all of that wonderful pressured motivational emotion of frustration! Convert it to action.

Once your list is compiled (keep this list running for at least 1 week), choose the one item that makes your blood boil!

- The one item: buy my coaching because I shot my video in front of a rented Lambo.
- The one item: the ignorant, incompetent decision-maker who leads the project.
- The one item: the client's niece completed a graphic design course and said, "Those are the wrong color palettes."
- The one time: "We'll check with our focus group."
- The one item: "I need it yesterday, but I won't respond to your email for three weeks and then ….Why didn't I have it yesterday?!"

It's **THE ONE THING** that you can no longer let slide in your industry or at least in your company.

If you had a gargoyle to perch yourself upon one stormy night, you'd yell out into the great expanse:

THIS INDUSTRY WILL RUE THE DAY IT EVER _____! This is your battle call, your call to action, **THE EXCLAMATION** of the change you will create. With each utterance, it should motivate you, fi re you up, make your blood boil, and create action.

Fill in the blank, and you will have the start of your **EXCLAMATION**, which will become a stepping stone in Step 5 of becoming a true MSV.

CHAPTER 9

STEP #4 THE MADNESS

"Madness is like gravity, all it needs is a little push"
— ***The Joker, The Dark Knight***

Now that we have identified the atrocities you will no longer tolerate in your industry, let's identify the madness that the consumers of your industry's products and services (a.k.a.: *your clients and potential clients*) will no longer accept.

Faithful MSV readers of Volume 1 (currently boasting a 4.7-star rating on Amazon) will recognize the importance of "Breaking Broca," a.k.a. Getting the bored, apathetic critic in your brain that filters thousands of daily messages to say "Wait …. What?!"

Aporia is a covert and clever way to shatter that mental autopilot. It was used by Socrates and other ancient philosophers to describe the moment in a dialogue when someone realizes they don't actually know what they thought they knew.

Aporia is "The Villain's Whisper." And now we're going to drag it into the spotlight right alongside The Joker and Batman.

Convinced the only thing that separates him from Batman is "one bad day," The Joker doesn't try to overpower Bats. He uses aporia. He gets into his head. He makes Batman question the very foundation of his alliance with law and order by pointing out how the police with whom Bats has an uneasy alliance would simply throw him away the second anything went astray.

"To them, you're just a freak... like me."

(You and I, we're not so different!)

It hits. Because deep down, Batman knows it's true.

That's aporia. It's not arguing. It's not persuading. It's creating a moment of mental vertigo. A crack in the armor. A whisper of doubt that unravels everything.

Aporia is not, "You're wrong."

Aporia is, "What if you were right... But in the worst way possible?"

Marketing books preach alignment. "Mirror your customer. Match their values. Meet them where they are."

Snooze.

Marketing Supervillains don't align. We disrupt.

Alignment-based marketing says, "Hey, I get you. I see where you're coming from. Let's walk this path together." It looks for empathy, resonance, and rapport.

Aporia-based marketing kicks the door in and says, "You're wrong, but in a way that's going to blow your mind and make you question everything you thought you knew."

Which one gets remembered?

Which one *starts* movements?

Alignment-based marketing is looking for a pat on the head.

Aporia-based marketing is how you steal the crown.

Let's see how a few legendary MSV brands did exactly that.

In 2014, Nickel Bank of France faced a population of people who assumed banking just wasn't for them. 255 banks in the nation, and every single one required both a large down payment and an in-person appointment to open an account.

People wrote banking off as exclusive to the affluent, as well as too inconvenient. So they stayed away and kept their money under their mattresses.

Wielders of aporia show prospects that they're not crazy for being frustrated; they're just victims of a broken system. Nickel Bank handed those people the detonator.

What the world believed:

"Banking is for rich people with time to kill."

What average marketers did:

"We're better bankers! Look at these happy people in our modern lobbies!"

What Nickel did:

They leaned into the skepticism. They said, "You're right. Traditional banks are a pain in the ass."

So they launched with:

- $20 account openings
- No appointments
- Bank-in-a-box kits from your local deli
- Tagline: "Nickel is the account for everyone."

They didn't fight the perception. They shattered the category. In 2017, a mere few years later, Nickel was acquired in what is considered one of the top 20 most important fintech acquisition deals in Europe (source Sifted). Despite the acquisition, Nickel retained its brand, independence, and market differentiator.

While bank marketing might not quench your creative thirst, perhaps our next example will.

Yellow Tail wines faced madness in their industry when they learned that a significant portion of adults had left wine behind, feeling "Wine was a turnoff. It's pretentious and too difficult to appreciate - not fun ... "

What the world believed:

"Wine is snobby, pretentious, and not fun."

What average marketers did:

"Not us! Look at our slightly more relatable wine snobs laughing on a beach!"

What Yellow Tail did:

They validated the disdain. Then invited people in.

Tagline: "Yellow Tail tastes like fun."

They didn't try to make wine more serious. They made it less. Within a decade, Yellow Tail carved out its market and became the number one imported wine in the U.S.

And finally, we have Planet Fitness.

Planet Fitness didn't whisper into the marketplace, *"We're a gym too, but we're cleaner and friendlier."* Nah. They rolled up with a megaphone and said:

"You're right. Gym culture *does* suck."

That, right there, is pure aporia. They acknowledged the discomfort people already felt; the intimidation, the meathead bro culture, the silent judgment dripping off every glistening bicep and said, *"Let's torch that entire paradigm."*

They didn't *align* with the current gym narrative. They **challenged it.** They **subverted expectations** by creating:

- A **Judgement-Free Zone®**
- **No grunting, no flexing,** and a **Lunk Alarm** that publicly shames gym egos
- Free **bagel and pizza days**
- Low prices and no pressure to "level up"

They positioned themselves as the **anti-gym gym,** and in doing so, **made everyone else look outdated, elitist, or just tone-deaf.**

And it worked like a damn charm.

In each case, aporia wasn't just a strategy. It was a superpower.

They didn't fight the madness. They agreed with it, leaned into it, and gave it just enough of a push to send their prospects tumbling down the rabbit hole. These brands *didn't win* by being better. They won by being **different** in a way that felt **emotionally validating** to a large, ignored audience.

That's how you create a new category.

That's how you sell from the shadows.

Aporia. The Joker doesn't tell Batman he's wrong. He makes him doubt he was ever right.

That's aporia, your entry point, your open window.

Now give it a little push.

APORIA EXERCISE:

MSV Breakdown: Utilize the chart below and insert your brand. Replace all of the alignment-based factors with what everyone else in your industry feels and says. Then figure out how to utilize aporia-based tactics to help differentiate your messaging in the marketplace.

	Aporia-Based (Planet Fitness)	Alignment-Based (Typical Gyms)
Tone	Subversive, challenging	Supportive, agreeable
Message	"You're right to hate gyms."	"Gyms are good, and we're a great one."
Audience Tactic	Weaponizes discontent	Mirrors beliefs
Emotional Trigger	Relief, surprise, rebellion	Safety, trust, motivation
Category Positioning	Creates a new subcategory (Anti-Gym)	Lives in the same old gym category
Result	Market domination	Market saturation

YOUR BRAND:

	Aporia-Based (Your Brand)	Alignment-Based (Your Competitors)
Tone		
Message		
Audience Tactic		
Emotional Trigger		
Category Positioning		
Result		

CHAPTER 10

STEP #5 THE SACRIFICE (THE BLOFELD PLOY REVISITED)

"The Culprit Is Known To Me. I Have Decided On The Appropriate Action."

— Ernst Stavro Blofeld

Walter White and Jesse Pinkman sit nervously at the edge of oblivion. Behind them, the cold presence of Mike Ehrmantraut simmers like a coiled viper. Across the room, Gus Fring, the gold standard of calculated villainy, watches in silence, flanked by his enforcer, Victor.

Walter pleads. Jesse twitches. Tension builds in the air like a snake tightening around its prey.

And then **SLICE.**

Not Jesse. Not Walter. But Victor. The henchman. The one who *thought* he was indispensable.

The message is clear: **Gus isn't playing.**

He doesn't explain. He doesn't raise his voice. He just drops the box cutter, straightens his tie, and walks away with the cold-blooded command:

"Get back to work."

What does this scene from Vince Gilligan's *Breaking Bad* have to do with becoming a Marketing Supervillain?

Everything.

This is what screenwriters call **The Blofeld Ploy.** Named after the legendary Bond villain Ernst Stavro Blofeld, it's the moment a true villain makes an example of someone expendable to elevate their credibility, tighten their inner circle, and assert complete control.

No, you don't need to off Carol in HR (though she knows what she did).

But you *do* need to start killing off your **worst clients** (ideologically, of course).

Who Deserves the Box Cutter?

We all talk about ideal clients: high-ticket, high-vibe, high-responsibility, drama-free unicorns. But how often do you define your *anti-client*?

- Ghosts your meetings

- Pays late (if at all)

- Constantly "just wants one more change"

- Thinks they're the expert, but has no data to back it up

- Makes you question your life choices

You know the type. (You probably have their emails starred in red):

MS. *"I don't see what I want, but I'll know it when I see it"* Now you see her, now you don't.

MR. Hush-Hush He likes NDA's more than he likes movement or results. In his case, NDA means No Decisions or Action.

MR. Bookie Client He wants to know precisely what his initial investment will yield once your marketing is completed, and wants to hold you to it. One thing his investment will no longer yield is doing business with you.

MRS. Brain Picker - *Mrs. Brain Picker She's easy to identify. "Can I pick your brain?" In other words, "I want consulting but I don't want to pay you." More like, "Can I pick your pocket?"*

Proud Aunts or Uncles *They have a niece or nephew who is "pretty creative" and has feedback for your recent designs.*

The harsh truth is this:

If you tolerate them, you teach your prospective clients that your time and talent are up for negotiation.

Villains don't ask for permission. Villains **establish terms.**

This isn't about arrogance, it's about clarity. It's about sending a signal to the market that your elevated skill sets are for those who *deserve* them.

The Chain Reaction of Power

"But wait," I hear your inner hero whisper. "How can I afford to drop clients when I still need to eat?"

Easy, my supervillain-in-training. Follow the formula:

1. You want to choose better clients.

2. But choice is impossible without *volume*. A healthy pool to pick from.

3. Volume requires **lead gen.**

4. Lead gen is powered by **marketing.**

5. But in a sea of noise, marketing is dead without **differentiation.**

And here's the kicker (most people miss):
Differentiation is not additive. It's reductive.
You don't stand out by piling on more features, services, or buzzwords. You stand out by *cutting away the noise.*
You **sacrifice** the weak clients. You **eliminate** what dilutes your power. You become **razor sharp.**
Like Gus with the box cutter, you *show* the world, not *tell* it, you mean business. You lead by example.
If you want to be irresistible to the right audience, be *repellent* to the wrong one.
Gus didn't give speeches. He didn't send Victor to HR.
He acted. With clarity. With conviction. With **discipline.**
You must do the same.
Because in villainy and branding alike, **more is not better. Better is better.**
So sharpen the blade. Define your enemies.
And start making sacrifices.

CHAPTER 11

STEP #6 THE AFTERMATH

"I became insane, with long intervals of horrible sanity."
— Edgar Allan Poe

astly, when a master supervillain strikes in Gotham City, Batman and Commissioner Gordon usually have an idea of who's behind the crime. Patterns emerge, signature styles reveal themselves, and big things like a bank heist don't come from two-bit crooks. Those heists have masterminds behind them.

Become that mastermind of your industry. Leave your unique signature on every interaction with a client and every piece of work you produce.

Just like the Riddler leaving his signature question mark calling card at the scene, you want your work to be instantly recognizable. People should exclaim, "Oh, that's so-and-so's project, I can tell from a mile away." Your craft, your message and your impact should be unmistakable. You want your signature to be so distinct that even the blind superhero, Daredevil, can see it.

While it may not be as prolific as Walter and Jesse's blue meth, your signature style should be recognizable from afar. But be forewarned, it's not about gimmicks. It's about essence. You are not performing a child's cheap magic trick; you are the consummate magician. What you do is real magic.

What do you bring to the table that no one else can? What calling card do you leave on every project? If you're just another interchangeable cog in the machine, easily swapped out, then you're expendable. And that, my dear villain, is a fate worse than death. If you are a generalist who says Yes to every scheme, every heist, or every client that comes through the door, you're just a common, everyday bit player. You're never going to get a starring role. You're cannon fodder, a henchman at best, and, let's be real, henchmen don't get their names on the marquee. Can you name even one of Mr. Freeze's sidekicks?

When you hit the launch button and the public sees your latest project, how will they know you are the evil genius behind it? Will it be unmistakably you, or could it have been done by any run-of-the-mill agency, consultant, or creator? That's the true test of mastery.

Going deep on your selected expertise is a great way to become famous … or, even better, infamous.

Infamy is where the real power lies. Anyone can be well-liked. Anyone can play it safe and blend in. But history doesn't remember those who played it safe and bent the knee. It writes about those who bent the world to their will. Those who set the terms rather than follow them. They are the legends, and their work is whispered about long after they're gone.

And let's not forget, the greatest villains are not just known for their deeds, but for their aesthetic. Their presence. Their essence.

Think of The Joker's purple suit, Hannibal Lecter's chilling calm, and Darth Vader's heavy breathing. Their legend isn't just built on their actions. They have an identity. They have their brand.

What's yours? Can I recognize your stamp from afar? Does your industry exclaim, "Oh, that's a [insert your last name]"?

If you haven't yet cultivated your signature, fear not. Today is your day. Today, you will start to define your unique style, your calling card, and your one-of-a-kind stamp. Do what the greats do. Obsess over every detail. How you speak. How you present. How you execute. Make it yours, and make it unmistakable. Your brand is not just a costume you put on when you are in front of a client. It is who you are … all of the time. If they can't spot you from across the room, across the internet, across the world, you don't exist. And in this game, being invisible means you've already lost.

PART 2

BUILDING YOUR SUPERVILLAIN FRAMEWORK

CHAPTER 12

WHERE DO YOU GET YOUR IDEAS?

"You're not out of ideas... You're out of perspective."
— Marketing Supervillain Doctrine, Section 3.2

Norm Macdonald is inarguably one of the funniest comedians to ever live. The guy was so funny, unique and engaging that I would, without exaggeration, intensely listen to his recap of how he prepared breakfast that day.

He could tell you how he toasted bread, and you'd listen like it was a TED Talk. The man could casually describe making eggs and somehow still land a joke about death, gambling, or Germans. Why? Because Norm had something rare:

A unique framework—a unique way of interpreting the world.

Not just punchlines. Not just jokes. A lens so distinct, you could almost predict how he'd react to anything... and yet you still couldn't wait to hear it.

Norm had a short-lived podcast where his sidekick, Adam Egrit, as a bit of a prank, would lob the same ridiculous question to their often A-list guests:

"Where do you get your ideas from?"

It's such a tired question, right? But it's also a fascinating one when you really think about it. Where does anyone get their ideas?

Imagine your favorite comic, someone whose voice is unmistakable, who has a completely unique perspective, commenting on your industry.

What would George Carlin say about influencer marketing?

How would Anthony Jeselnik roast your category's sacred cow?

How would Bill Burr explode over a boardroom filled with acronym-slinging consultants?

That's the magic.

Great comedians don't just tell jokes. They expose the cracks in logic and light them on fire.

Their gift isn't just cleverness, it's perspective.

Their framework is so strong, they can talk about anything... and it still feels like **them**.

Now, let's talk about the other side of the coin: the rookie comic. You've seen them. Scattered jokes, no real voice. They might get a few chuckles, but you walk away remembering... nothing.

Why? Because there's no throughline.

They're playing wide, not deep.

They perform many jokes for a few people.

Pros perform a few jokes for many.

That's not just a stand-up lesson. It's a branding law.

The novice dabbles in ever-changing topics. The pro dominates from a unique perspective.

Let's get real. As business owners or creators, we don't have to stand on a stage every night, but we do feel that creeping anxiety when our social media accounts, blogs, or platforms go silent for too long. So, what do we do? We churn out content for content's sake.

You've seen it. Hell, you may have posted it:

"5 Tips for Better SEO"

"Why Email Marketing Still Matters in 2025"

"What I Learned from [Insert Buzzword-titled Book]"

There's no bite. No spark. No soul.

Just digital tofu. Bland. Forgettable. Drifting through LinkedIn like tumbleweeds.

Now imagine this:

Instead of scrambling for your next piece of content, it erupts from you.

Why? Because you've discovered your **EXCLAMATION**, your "This F'N Industry of Mine" statement from Chapter 8!

That one frustrating, infuriating, hilarious or shameful truth that you can't ignore any longer.

The thing you know, deep in your villainous core, is wrong with the system.

Once you articulate it, the floodgates open.

Because now, you're not just a talking head, you're a fire-breathing viewpoint.

Your content becomes less like "posting" and more like broadcasting from your lair.

You don't chase relevance. Relevance comes looking for you.

People start asking, "What do you think about this?"

Now you're in demand.

This isn't just a way to stand out. It's your infinite creativity glitch.

Your perspective defines your framework, and your framework births content that only you can create. It's no longer about writing for the sake of it; it's about building a body of work that resonates, challenges, and connects. Your views are welcomed and sought-after because they are different from those of the masses. They are insightful in only a way you can curate.

Suddenly, every:

Industry trend
Dumb client request
Viral news moment
Overused buzzword

...is an opportunity to apply your lens and say something that only you could say.

You're no longer writing content, you're building a worldview.
A worldview that:
Attracts loyal fans
Repels the wrong ones
Establishes authority without having to beg for it

From there, everything changes.

CHAPTER 13

YOU AND I... WE'RE COMPLETELY DIFFERENT!

"Revolutions start with one person willing to be misunderstood."

— MSV Doctrine, Article XIII, Section BURN

Remember aporia? That covert tactic where we challenged the beliefs prospects already held? Yeah, forget it. This is not the time for aporia. This is the time to draw your sword, plant your flag, and let the world know:

You think and act completely differently from anyone else in your field.

This isn't the Joker whispering a dark truth. This is Bane snapping the old system over his knee like Batman's spine.

Take Norm Macdonald and his signature anti-punchlines. I didn't love him because he was relatable. I loved him because he was an anomaly. His perspective. His tempo. He made the entire room uncomfortable, then made you fall in love with the discomfort.

Norm perfectly demonstrates the power of differentiation. He is unapologetic, fearless and, as a result, breaks Broca.

When you claim radical difference, you're exposing your audience to an entirely different perspective, often reaching into the deepest fears and frustrations that they haven't yet admitted to themselves. On the other hand, when you utilize Aporia, you're shaking prospects out of their shallow assumptions.

Ask yourself:

Why does the way your industry operates piss you off so much?

- Is it a clash in values?
- A betrayal of what you know to be right?
- Or does it go deeper?

Let's say you're a marketer who loathes clients chasing vanity metrics.

You could stop at:

- "It's short-term thinking."
- "It's not financially sustainable."

But ask again. WHY?

- Because you were burned once.
- Because your better ways are most often ignored.
- Because your integrity can't co-sign hollow wins.

Keep asking until you hit the root. And when you do?
That's your war cry.

Make the Contrast Loud

Now, make that difference *unignorable.*

Drop a contrasting statement so bold, so heretical to your industry's norms, that your audience can't help but ask:

"Wait... why would they say that?"

Examples:

- "We don't take small-budget social media campaigns. Period."
- "We don't track Likes. We track brand loyalty over years."
- "We don't do trendy SEO hacks. We build category leaders."

You're not just planting a flag. You're *scorching the earth* around it.

This Is Your MSV Exclamation

This isn't venting. This is your **rally cry.** This is the message that magnetizes your tribe. This is the thing your true believers will repeat to their friends.

If your MSV Exclamation doesn't make you a little nervous to say out loud, it's not bold enough.

People who share your frustrations will find you. Those who don't? They were never yours to begin with.

Whatever your **EXCLAMATION** is, say it like you mean it. Say it until they either follow you or fear you.

Here are some example exclamations from different industries:

Business Coach

"In this F'N industry, everyone's selling a 'dream life' without the work it takes to get there. I build habits, not fantasies."

Content Writers

"In this F'N industry, creativity is sacrificed at the altar of the algorithm. I write to move people, not just machines."

Fashion

"In this F'N industry, size inclusivity is a buzzword. I design for real bodies, not runway fantasies."

Finance

"In this F'N industry, everyone chases flashy investments. I build boring, consistent wealth. The kind that actually lasts."

Education

"In this F'N industry, test scores matter more than curiosity. I teach people how to love learning again."

Fitness

"In this F'N industry, we worship six-pack abs. I teach sustainable health, not punishment."

Now it's your turn. Pick a fight with the status quo. Then shout your MSV Exclamation from the rooftops.

This is how you stop being just another option. This is how you become **the only option**.

Go forth. Build your army. Burn the playbook.

CHAPTER 14

THE GHOST IN THE MACHINE: WHAT IFS? WHAT IS!

A mind once infected with doubt is a garden where regret takes root.

— MSV Psy-Ops Strategy Guide

So... back to those lost prospects of mine. The ones who "went in another direction."

Marketing Supervillains don't just want to win the account. We want to linger. We want to infect their minds so thoroughly that any campaign without us feels like a knockoff. We want to haunt.

I used to just want to outshine their new agency. To prove I was the better choice. But that's amateur hour. That's what stereotypical heroes do, concern themselves with public opinion. No. I'm not motivated. I'm hell-bent. I want them haunted.

Haunted by the creeping realization that maybe, just maybe, my lost prospects made a fatal error in judgment. That maybe the guy in the suit with the milquetoast pitch deck wasn't the marketing messiah they thought.

How would I accomplish this haunting? How do I ensure that at 3 AM, they lie in their bed wide-eyed awake and sweating, replaying, like a child's playground taunt, the cursed nursery rhyme:

"What if I had hired Jesse?"

No one lies awake at night feeling smug about saving a few bucks or choosing the safe, predictable path. No one breaks into a cold sweat thinking about the money they didn't spend.

People lose sleep over missed opportunities. Over risks they didn't take. Over the one mad genius they brushed off, the one who could've pulled off the impossible.

This is no longer about being better.

It's about being unforgettable.

It's about the gaping hole that is left by your absence.

A killer list of previous clients, raving testimonials and a beautiful portfolio aren't going to get it done. Those are the table stakes just to get you dealt into the conversation.

Now that you're holding the cards, it's time to let them know you are the rounder (a player who skillfully exploits the "angles" of the game to make a living at the poker table).

In today's day and age, it's simple to craft perceptual equity in expertise. Pitching a cyber security firm? Have ChatGPT author you a book on the subject. Perform a 5-minute pitch at your local chamber of commerce, snap a photo of yourself on stage, then update that LinkedIn profile of yours with a dazzling title: Cyber Security Marketing Expert, Author and Keynote Speaker, and you're off to the races.

Your pitch will undoubtedly hold a little more weight compared to the competition, but that is amateur hour. We're MSVs, we're crafting nightmares, not vanity-laced e-books.

You don't just want prospects to remember you. You want them to doubt everything else that comes after you.

A mind once infected with doubt is a garden where regret takes root.

Thought Experiments To Get The Ball Rolling

A.K.A. Psychic Warfare 101
Loss of Market Mythology

- **With You:** They would have become legends and they would have achieved cultural relevance.

- **Without You:** They're just a LinkedIn post and they achieved a few Likes and a pat on the back from the board.

- **Final Result:** From your vantage point, you can accurately predict the moment the algorithm buries them alive.

Loss of Cult Status

- **With You:** They would have gotten perspective forged in the fire of how people really talk and feel and receive the truth, even if it were harsh.

- **Without You:** They settle for messaging born in the air-conditioned glow of a two-way mirror room where Karen from Milwaukee shrugs at their taglines.

- **Final Result:** They bask in the safe, soft, comforting answers a mom gives when you ask, *"How does my outfit look?"* Their pathetic rally cry rallies no one, so they wallow in mediocrity, claiming "marketing doesn't work."

Loss of Cultural Gravity

- **With You:** Instead of riding a wave, they would have created the current that others would have looked to for inspiration.

- **Without You:** They are forever two steps behind, chasing hashtags and hoping to stay relevant by mimicking competitors.

- **Final Result:** In addition to losing the cultural gravity you would have achieved for the brand, they lose the sense of gravity altogether. Within months (or weeks), when the enthusiasm of a new campaign wears off, they are left floating adrift like an astronaut whose spacecraft ran out of gas.

Loss of First-Mover Fearlessness

- **With You:** The industry would've whispered their name with a mix of admiration and fear. They would've owned the narrative and set the pace, forcing others to play catch-up.

- **Without You:** They blend into the background noise, indistinguishable from the imitators they once mocked, now just spectators in a game they should've been dominating.

- **Final Result:** The crown was within reach, but instead of seizing it, they handed it to someone braver.

Loss of Momentum

- **With You:** Momentum would've become their most powerful asset, as they would've blasted out of the gates, igniting their brand with rocket fuel.

- **Without You:** They opted for a scenic route with someone still checking the map.

- **Final Result:** Their launch window closed the moment they picked a "safe" option. While they crawl through strategy decks and revisions, the world moves on... and their audience forgets they ever cared.

Loss of the Marketing Weapon No One Else Has

- **With You:** They would've wielded a marketing weapon forged from obsession, insight, and a touch of beautiful madness. Their competitors would've scrambled to figure out how the hell they pulled it off.

- **Without You:** They picked the agency equivalent of a butter knife in a gunfight. Now they blend right back into the noise, armed with the same bland tactics everyone else is recycling.

- **Final Result:** You were their unfair advantage. A secret weapon. A once-in-a-career opportunity to dominate. Now? That weapon walks away, still fully loaded... and possibly pointed at them next time.

Loss of Being Remembered As the One Who Got It Right

- **With You:** They would've made the bold call that others looked back on and said, "That's when everything changed."

- **Without You:** They made the safe choice, the one that got lost in the shuffle and footnotes, now reduced to a passing mention in a case study no one reads.

- **Final Result:** They had the chance to make history. Instead, they chose someone who promised "consistency." History doesn't remember consistency. It remembers the bold.

Forget winning - craft your pitch to linger:

- Make one bold prediction.
- Offer one "impossible-to-source-anywhere-else" insight.
- Warn them of a future storm only you can see.
- Use a metaphor so memorable it shows up in their dreams.
- Leave behind an artifact. A physical or digital item that becomes a totem of doubt.
- Make them wonder. Not about how much it would cost them to work with you, but how much it would cost them if they let this opportunity slip.

They might forget your pitch deck. But they'll never forget the stories you told.

CHAPTER 15:

DEATH BY A THOUSAND "TWEAKS"

"There comes a time when 'being professional'
is just code for 'dying quietly.'
You don't have to."

— MSV Doctrine, Article XVIII

I'm sure you've heard it before.

"It's not personal."

Oh, but it is.

If you're worth your weight as a professional marketer, every project is a piece of you. You take pride in all you do. Your design isn't just a layout; it's a declaration. Your copy isn't just messaging; it's philosophy. When they ask you to change it, it feels like they are rejecting it, and, as such, they are rejecting you.

It's most often delivered with some level of couth/compassion/gentleness: "Let's try a version with Comic Sans," or perhaps more insultingly: *"My nephew said this reminds him of a funeral."* They are ignorant because they think they are just commenting about the work, not you. But you know better. You *feel* it. Your work is you.

This is where most creatives fold. They start gaslighting themselves.

"Maybe I am overreacting... Maybe that change isn't so bad... Maybe this is just how the process works..."

But deep down, you know the truth: every "tiny revision" is a dagger to the identity you've cultivated. They didn't just defang your design. They neutered your purpose.

Section I: The Myth of Collaboration

They say they want a "collaborative process," but what they really mean is "I want to be in control, but I don't want the blame if it fails."

True collaboration is rare. Most of the time, you're an assassin-for-hire with your hands tied behind your back in a room full of spectators telling you how to aim.

And the second you push back? You're labeled difficult, arrogant, or not a "team player."

You know deep inside, in order to truly be successful, you need the leeway to lead, but most projects lack a true leader who can take both the glory, and the potential pain of failure.

Section II: Emotional Collateral Damage

Let's talk about the psychological toll on your well-being. You start doubting yourself. You become gun-shy with bold ideas. You sand the edges off your brilliance until everything you produce is safe, beige, inoffensive. Your work no longer has edges. Everything is a gentle curve so as not to catch itself on the fabric of your client. It's toothless.

Your art becomes a hostage to consensus, your vision is diluted in a pool of "just to be safe" decisions. Your body of professional work or worse, your version of Michelangelo's *David* is chiseled down to a hulking monument to compromise.

Before you know it, you've stopped bringing your A-game to the table. Why would you? They're just going to feed it into the meat grinder anyway.

Being a Marketing Supervillain isn't just about big ideas or bold branding. It's about defending the sanctity of your vision. It's about making sure your work doesn't just exist, but thrives—undiluted, untamed, unmistakably *you*.

Every change they suggest is an invitation to compromise.

So what do we do?

Still wondering about when it's time to finally burn the bridge?

Before you flick that match, read on to the next chapter, my villainous trainee.

CHAPTER 16

STACKING THE DECK IN YOUR FAVOR

"Normal is not something to aspire to, it's something to get away from."

— Jodie Foster

The number one question I get asked after I give my keynote while on the Travelling Supervillain Roadshow is "Now that I've accepted my role as an MSV, what do I do at that inevitable, pivotal point when a client or a stakeholder pushes back on my ideas?" (It's usually not stated so eloquently, and more often has undertones of frustration and angst, sounding more like "They still won't listen to me! What the #&% do I do now??"

"Do I flip the table over and walk away?"

"Do I fold and chase the buck?"

"How do I continue to put food on the table?"

"What am I saying wrong, that they don't get?"

These are all valid questions, and the answer is: If your relationship with your client has gotten to this point, something went wrong long ago.

Let's take a small tangent. Imagine you are fumbling around your supervillain's lair one night and you stub your pinky toe. You nurse it for quite a while, but 3 months later, it still hurts, so you visit your general practitioner.

Your relationship with your family doctor is similar to your relationship with clients. Decent rapport, you've even referred your doctor to other friends and family members, just as clients (hopefully) have done for you in the past.

Your trusted doctor looks at your foot for exactly 30 seconds and breaks the bad news: "We have to amputate." Now, even though you've used this doctor for years, good rapport aside, you'll likely get a second opinion before lopping off a part of your body.

So you ask around, and someone you know has an in with "The Pinky Toe Guy." This doctor is known as Dr. Pinky---he's been on Oprah, and he's even written a book on the little piggy that cried wee wee wee all the way home.

You have no history with this doc, no rapport. Thirty seconds after looking at your foot, he breaks the same news: Amputation time.

Are you more likely or less likely to put greater weight in this doctor's prognosis? Of course you will, but why?

It's simply because Dr. Pinky Toe designed his own packaging and aura. Expectations were set long before you even met him. You anticipated that he was the specialist of specialists and his verdict was the final word on the subject matter. And, most importantly, you don't even know if in fact he is the highest qualified person to make a diagnosis! Did you take the time to see if he graduated top in his Pinky Toe class or at the very bottom? Did he even go to Pinky Toe University? The persona he created told that story, accurately or inaccurately, to you.

So, how do you set expectations before you even walk into the room?

You build your villainous legend. You develop such a vivid, powerful, differentiated brand persona, that your very name invokes a feeling.

Consider this: If you were planning on robbing a liquor store and needed a partner in crime, would you ask the Joker? Probably not. Based on the limited scope of the project, he'd laugh you out of Gotham City. The Joker has the aura of an evil mastermind who would never waste his valuable time on such trivial, small-minded heists.

The grandiose aura of which we speak, similar to the doctor, was created entirely by the Joker himself. He had already set expectations on the scope of projects he was willing to entertain way before you approached him with the idea. No one gave him permission to be so arrogant or steadfast, nor did he ever ask for it. (Could you imagine a *supervillain* asking for permission!?) He's established an actual set point for what projects are worthy of his efforts and energy, simply because that's what he wanted. Period. End of story.

MSV Exercise

Let's get tactical.

1. Define Your Superpower.

Your superpower is the feeling your work evokes in the people who experience it. Notice: it's not the feeling *you* evoke. It's all about the work. It's not about you. Separating yourself from your work is a superpower in its own right, and an important one at that, perhaps the most important. Also, notice I didn't just say, "when the people *see* it." You are an MSV. People do not just see your work, they *experience* it. It's visceral and, as such, unforgettable. They may gasp, they may cry, they may get angry. It's all great, because they are *feeling something*.

Think: *"I'm the guy who makes you rethink and refeel everything you thought you knew." Or, "I turn beige brands into bold cults."*

2. Build Your Lair.

This is your environment. Your touchpoints. Your website, your slides, your proposals, your social feed. Every inch should drip with consistency, clarity, and flair. Is it generic? Then it's gone. Imagine walking into Peloton's HQ and seeing a fridge full of sugary sodas or pulling up to the Patagonia corporate office parking lot and seeing a dozen Hummers parked up front. How about the chances of spotting that "Hang In There!" poster of the kitten clinging to a rope for dear life in a Tough Mudder employee's cubicle? These brands have created an image and an ethos so strong that you can automatically assume some of the finer characteristics of their lairs without even visiting.

Every villain's lair is memorable. Yours should be too, and it should inspire *you*.

Think: *Eliminate anything that makes you look available, affordable, or desperate. You're building mystique, not running a Groupon special.*

3. Create an Entry Protocol.

High-value characters don't take meetings with everyone. They have a protocol. So should you. Maybe it's an in-depth questionnaire. Maybe it's a paid consultation before the real work begins. Maybe it's simply a custom, snarky autoresponder that subtly reminds them they're lucky to be in your inbox. Creating a gatekeeper, whether it is digital or human, adds infinite value to your time and filters out those who would waste it. Access to the best is a privilege for the few.

"Thanks for reaching out. If this is about a beige brochure or your cousin's DJ logo, I'm probably not your guy. But if you want to shake your industry to its core, tell me more..."

4. Don't Create Content. Evangelize A Revolution.

Thought leadership is for heroes, desperate to be seen as wise, cautious, and palatable. But you're not a hero! You're a disruptor, an instigator, a Marketing Supervillain. MSVs don't dabble in "content creation" like everyone else trapped in the hamster wheel of the algorithm. You aren't here to appease LinkedIn or gain lukewarm applause from your peers. You're here to broadcast doctrine. Every word you write, every pixel you publish, every breath you put into a podcast should be treated like a manifesto: bold, blasphemous, and bound to rattle cages. Don't comment on the industry. Set it ablaze. Your lens isn't just unique, it's weaponized. You're not writing blog posts; you're etching commandments into stone. Stop adding to the noise. Instead, be the thunder that makes the herd scatter. MSVs don't chase relevance; they shape reality.

5. Collect Proof of Power.

Build a Hall of Fame of your victories. Case studies? Sure, but not the plain old vanilla type. Think bloody capes of vanquished heroes in a trophy case. Tell the story of the impossible thing you pulled off. The industry norms you set on fire. The client who almost said No... and came back begging. Showcase testimonials from people who sound like they barely survived working with you... and would do it again.

Now it's your turn. Utilize all of the tips and steps laid out within this exercise and begin your own repackaging. Create your own aura of how you want to be viewed, perceived, or even felt in the market; there is literally no limit!

Extra Points:

Flip the Script on Your Shortcomings

Did you know Thomas Edison was painfully introverted? The man wasn't built for boardrooms or backslaps. When investors came knocking, hopeful, checkbooks twitching, Tom would feel the panic rise in his chest like a live wire. He'd invent excuses (how appropriate) just to escape into the sanctuary of his lab. He thought this flaw, this "weakness," would ruin him. Social anxiety, he feared, would be the death of his career and any hope of financial success.

But then the tables turned.

What Edison thought was a liability became his superpower. The harder it was to get face time with him, the more the people wanted it. The more he hid in his lair, the more mythic it became. Investors whispered about the work going on behind those locked doors. Rumors swirled. Mystique bloomed.

He didn't have to sell himself anymore. He became the thing people wanted access to.

Lucky for Edison, this happened organically for him, and the rest is quite literally history. MSVs don't have to let nature run its course. What aspect from the above exercises could a forceful villainous hand put into motion to cover up what you perceive as a weakness?

PART 3

YOUR SUPERVILLAIN MANIFESTO

CHAPTER 17

THE MANIFESTO

"Every great villain lives by a code.
Yours just hasn't been written yet."

The word "manifesto," much like the label "supervillain," has unjustly garnered a bad reputation. The agency R/GA recently tweeted, "Advertising is still the only place where writing a manifesto isn't a red flag," and this quote lives in my head rent-free.

At its core, a manifesto is nothing more than a public declaration of how you move through the world. The code you abide by, the values you defend.

Your battle cry is your offensive game plan. As an MSV, you don't fight from the trenches. You wield your sword, your manifesto, rush to the front line, and cut through the noise of other marketers, screaming your truth.

It's your recipe for revolution.

Crafting a manifesto isn't easy. It's work – HARD work. If you are doing it correctly and effectively, you should sweat, struggle, and swear as you give birth to it. But for any Marketing Supervillain worth their salt, it's absolutely essential.

Why is a manifesto mission critical to your success?

Your manifesto is the physical manifestation of your inner Supervillain. It's your playbook, keeping you in alignment with your core values and villainous integrity, even when the going gets tough.

A Moral Compass When No One is Watching:

When temptation shows up in khakis with a charming smile, a thick wad of cash, and a "quick project" that promises easy wins, your manifesto becomes more than just words—it becomes armor. It gives you the strength to say "no" without flinching, without second-guessing, even when the offer is shiny, seductive, and no one else is around to see your decision. When there's no boardroom, no audience, and no accountability partner to keep you honest, your manifesto steps in. It reminds you who you are, what you stand for, and why you started this journey in the first place. It becomes your lighthouse in the fog of convenience, helping you reject anything misaligned with your values, even when that means walking away from what looks like a golden opportunity. Integrity doesn't announce itself—it's revealed in quiet, unglamorous moments. Your manifesto makes sure you're ready for them.

Here's a simple fact that many (dare I say most?) agency owners do not realize: *All* clients are not *your* clients. The challenge comes in identifying who is who. Your manifesto is your filter. It provides *objective* feedback in making a decision where subjectivity usually rules.

Focus and Power During Tough Times:
When in doubt, consult the code. When challenged, double down on it.

With your manifesto, you grow stronger, more focused, and more authentically aligned with the power of your vision. Your manifesto is a filter. It helps identify the right clients while deterring you from engaging with those who don't align with your values.

For example, clients sometimes ask me to clone a competitor's website, make a few changes, and call it a day. Could I do it? Of course. Previous to the birth of my MSV, I've done it countless times. But now, I turn down these requests, not because they're unethical (let's be honest, most website conversations start with "What other sites do you like?"), but because they insult my expertise.

How about my personal #1 most cringeworthy request from a client: "We want to look like those guys."

When businesses enter a new market, they often look to claw at market share by emulating a Super Brand—a dominant, well-resourced, highly visible leader in their space. These Super Brands are like superheroes; they have huge public favor, big muscles (i.e. big budgets), and a significant head start.

Supervillains don't play that game.

We don't try to outspend or outshine the big players on their terms. Instead, we use cunning, wit and strategy to outmaneuver them. Trying to go head-to-head with a Super Brand is a fool's errand, especially when you're under-resourced.

This ethos is encapsulated in the second principle of the Marketing Supervillain Manifesto:

"I am not here to do what has already been done."

At this stage of the game, taking on mindless, derivative projects feels like settling for mediocrity when I'm destined for mythology. My manifesto reminds me of that. It's not wallpaper. It's scripture.

Mine is encased in acrylic and bolted to the wall outside my office. Not for decoration. For defense. For declaration. For daily alignment. It is my armor.

My Manifesto is as Follows:

#1: **I HAVE A CONTRASTING PERSPECTIVE ON MY MARKETPLACE.**

I've tried the traditional path and, well, it simply wasn't right for me.

I am the catalyst of the REVOLUTION of my industry.

#2: **I AM NOT HERE TO DO WHAT HAS ALREADY BEEN DONE.**

I do not look to others for inspiration - others look to me.

#3: **I PAY NO ATTENTION TO GUARDRAILS.**

Guardrails are there to keep people on the paved road. I have no interest in following the same road as the masses. I pave my own pathway and lead the way for others by seeing the madness in my industry and reshaping it.

#4: **MY TACTICS WILL SURELY ATTRACT CRITICISM FROM THE AVERAGE MASSES.**

I accept these critiques. The unknowing always criticize that which they don't know or understand. That is their problem, not mine.

#5: I DO NOT MAKE EXCUSES.

I create new paradigms to get to the top and am willing to sacrifice to get there.

#6: I HAVE ZERO INTEREST IN CREATING DRAMA FOR THE SAKE OF DRAMA.

When I create drama, I create it for the sake of creating business.

#7. I WILL NOT CHANGE MY VISION TO MEET THE EXPECTATIONS OF THE WORLD.

I will change the world to match my vision.

CHAPTER 18

CRAFTING YOUR MANIFESTO

"You're either ALONE—or you're a LEADER.
There is no middle ground."

— The MSV Church Of The Converted Psalm 4:23

Ready to write your supervillain code?

Your Code isn't a mission statement. It's not corporate fluff. It's the gospel according to you—etched in stone, chiseled in rage, and lit with the fires of your originality.

As Marketing Supervillains, we are ahead of the curve. We see the cracks in the façade long before the building crumbles. Our ideas challenge the status quo. And that always, as it should, gets us labeled "too intense," "too idealistic," or "too much."

Let them talk.

As wrestling legend "Hot Rod" Rowdy Roddy Piper said, "People will love you for the same reason they hated you in the first place."

But that love only comes when you refuse to flinch, when you hold your ground, when you live by your code. Regardless whether they agree or not, people respect others with a clear code.

When the market finally realizes it doesn't *want* change, but desperately *needs* it, you will be ready.

And your manifesto will be the beacon in the night.

Let's get started:

It's time to truly embody/embrace your inner supervillain. Supervillains do not think small, and the creation of your code of ethics and aspirations as a market mover should be no different.

Think **aspirational**. Then **go bigger**.

These aren't mission statements, they are declarations for a new reality. Your next objective is to create the steps on how you get there.

STEP 1: BURN IT DOWN

Objective: Identify the exact moment you snapped.

Your "This F'N Industry of Mine" epiphany isn't a gripe, it's your *origin story*. It's when you saw the Matrix glitch. When you realized the people in charge were incompetent, spineless, or both.

Write it like a scar. *Don't intellectualize it. Bleed it out.*

Think About:

What's the moment you realized your industry was a farce? What idiocy made you clench your jaw? What betrayal, trend, or lie do you refuse to perpetuate? (If this feels familiar, it's because you've previously addressed it in Chapter 8: The Exclamation.)

Example:

I'm done explaining creative strategy to clients who picked their logo color because it "matches our couch."

STEP 2: DRAW YOUR LINES

Objective: Declare your non-negotiables.

These are the boundaries of your villain lair. Anyone who crosses them? Gone. Vaporized. These lines are sacred. Money, exposure or prestige can't buy their erasure.

Think About:

What clients, behaviors or requests have made you feel like a disposable vendor?

What work drained your soul, made you compromise your integrity, or forced you to silence your instincts?

What work will you never do again, no matter the payday?

Important: You must kill the voice whispering, "But what if they pay well?" That's not your voice. That's fear wearing a tie.

Example:

I no longer build websites for people who say, "I just need something simple."

STEP 3: CLAIM YOUR ZONE OF GENIUS

Objective: Own your dangerous brilliance without apologizing.

Most people dim their genius to make others comfortable. You don't.

This is where you take the weird, extreme, obsessive parts of your talent and weaponize them.

Think About:

What can you do in your sleep that others struggle with when fully caffeinated?

What dangerous idea would you build if you had no fear of judgment?

What is your unfair advantage?

Clarification:

"Loudly. With no disclaimers."

Do NOT add "But I still have room to grow."

Do NOT say "I try my best" or "I can probably help you with that, too."

Do NOT sand down your edges.

Examples:

I don't write copy. I inject ideas that hijack the limbic system.

I don't run campaigns. I architect cults.

STEP 4: BUILD YOUR WORLD

Objective: Declare the revolution you're engineering.

This is your vision for a better world, one built in your image. Not just for you, but for the tribe you're assembling. It's the cult. The cause. The dream you refuse to die without building.

Think About:

If you won, if you really won, what would change for your clients, industry, or culture?

What becomes obsolete? What becomes holy?

Examples:

I'm creating a future where genius misfits don't beg for permission; they own the room the moment they walk in.

I'm building a marketplace where weird wins, rebels rise, and being "too much" is necessary.

STEP 5: DISTILL THE MADNESS

Objective: Distill your entire villain origin, rebellion and revolution into 3–6 electric lines.

These are not "beliefs." They're laws. Use active voice. Be declarative. This is not a draft. It's your declaration of war.

Think About:

What do you know to be true, even if the industry hates it?

What would you scream from a rooftop?

What will you be remembered for?

Examples:

I believe vanilla brands deserve to die.

I don't market products. I create movements.

Authenticity isn't a tactic. It's a weapon.

I will not change my vision to meet the expectations of the world, instead, I will change the world to match my vision. (My personal favorite and #7 from my personal Supervillain Manifesto)

STEP 6: MAKE IT REAL

Objective: Give your Code a home.

If it lives in your notebook, it dies there. It must be public. Visible. Enshrined.

Think About:

Where will you see it every day?

Where should others see it and know they're either with you… or against you?

Examples:

Print it on a steel plaque for your office wall.

Make it the virtual background for Zoom and Teams calls.

Put it in the footer of your proposals.

Tattoo it. (Seriously.)

Make it a screensaver or your desktop wallpaper.

Read it before every strategy meeting to remember who the hell you are.

Remember, if it's not worth sharing, it's not worth writing.

Write the Code. Wield the Power.

PART 4

SUMMONING YOUR DARK MUSE:
CASE STUDIES

CHAPTER 19

READING TRENDS FOR FUN & PROFIT

"Only dead fish go with the flow."

— Malcolm Muggeridge

CASE STUDY 1:

Every trend swings like a wrecking ball; predictably, back and forth, destroying everything in its path until someone's brave enough to stop admiring the arc... and *grab the chain*. Not just to escape the cycle but to build something entirely new from the rubble.

There is one brand that didn't just break the system—it replaced it with a hallucinogenic fever dream. A network that built its empire on the backs of the bizarre, the broken, and the beautifully unmarketable: Adult Swim.

Since its unholy birth, Cartoon Network's programming block, Adult Swim has been the bleeding edge. An incubator of the experimental, the absurd, the gloriously unmarketable. It doesn't just push boundaries; it feeds them LSD, locks them in a basement, and films what happens next.

If you've created something so strange, so differentiated, so completely unfit for polite society that it deserves a bigger spotlight, then Adult Swim is your first call. The result? A devoted, frothing-at-the-mouth fanbase that would follow the network into a volcano if asked (and probably record it on VHS for aesthetic purposes).

Adult Swim didn't just swing the pendulum. It ripped the damn thing off its axis and launched it into another dimension.

So... where's the opportunity?

Enter Adult Swim comedian Joe Pera. In a realm dominated by nightmare-fuel animation, surrealist sketch comedy, and 4 am infomercial parodies that feel like the embodiment of a night terror, Joe Pera stands defiantly still. If Andy Kaufman's absurdity was dialed to an 11, Joe Pera dials it all the way down to a painfully awkward 1 and, in doing so, breaks the system.

Where others scream for attention, Joe whispers. While every producer tries to escalate the insanity, Joe parks himself in the mundane and makes it magic. In his universe, Sunday isn't for chaos; it's for taking Grandma to the hair salon. And damnit if it isn't mesmerizing to sit with him in the waiting room while retirees gossip about perms and politics.

Joe Pera is the anti-trend, the counterspell to the network's madness. And that's exactly why it works.

Adult Swim has built such a defined brand that creators and audiences alike can predict what's coming next. And when a brand becomes predictable, most rush to copy the formula. But the smarter move, the villainous move, is to flip the entire script. Poke fun at the system.

Lesson:

True brand power isn't about volume. It's about *contrast*.

Your Mission:

You don't always win by going bigger. Sometimes, you win by going weirder... and quieter. Whisper when they expect a roar. Let the world lean in. And when they do? Own the silence.

CHAPTER 20

THE DAY I GOT AWAY WITH IT

"Sometimes you don't ask for permission or forgiveness.
Sometimes... you just walk out with the shirt."

— Pulled from MSV interrogation footage

CASE STUDY 2:

Supervillains aren't typically known for small-time antics like shoplifting. We're more about "global disruption" than petty theft.

But dammit... I did it.

I stole.

I *loved* it.

And I tell the tale every chance I get.

Here's the kicker: the brand I stole from *wanted* me to do so.

Enter: **MSCHF**, the beautifully twisted art collective out of Brooklyn, New York. They're the punk rock prophets of the marketing world—blurring the line between commerce and commentary with every viral, subversive drop. These are the maniacs who created a microscopic Louis Vuitton-style handbag, smaller than a grain of sea salt ... and sold it for over $63,000. That's not a typo. That's gospel. That's MSV territory.

So when I caught wind that MSCHF, who are usually locked in their black-box fortress of secrecy, were doing a *physical* sale in NYC, I didn't walk. I *teleported*.

This was a rare chance to get hands-on with some of their overstock, a tactile piece of the anti-capitalist chaos they peddled. That's when I saw it: a stack of mysterious boxes.

Inside?

The legendary "Impossible Shirt." A Frankensteined garment stitched together from 10 different designer brand shirts. Capitalism was torn apart and reassembled into a single MSCHF-branded abomination. A wearable middle finger to consumerism.

Above the pile was a handwritten sign that read:

PLEASE

don't

STEAL

The word **DON'T** was written in ant-sized font, barely legible. Meanwhile, **PLEASE** and **STEAL** practically screamed in neon.

Was this ... an invitation? A challenge? A test?

This was *so* on-brand that it almost felt personal. Like the gods of absurdist marketing were whispering in my ear: *Go on. Do it. You know you want to.*

I paused for a split second.

Then said, "Screw it."

Grabbed a box.

And casually walked out.

No alarms. No resistance. Just a quiet thrill humming through my veins. For a moment, I felt like Danny Ocean with a duffel bag full of irony.

Later that night, a deep dive on Reddit confirmed what I suspected all along: *that was the point.* The whole stunt was intentional. MSCHF wanted to reward those who understood the brand deeply enough to act on instinct, to embrace the absurd, and break the unwritten rules of traditional retail.

Let that sink in: they turned a pile of unsold inventory into *a brand story.* A *ritual.* A *heist-worthy experience* that will be told and retold for years to come.

That, my friends, is how legends---and loyalty and MSVs---are born.

Lesson:

When your brand is bold enough, *every action becomes content.* Every touchpoint becomes a test. Give your audience a chance to prove they get you. The ones who pass? They become evangelists.

Your mission:

Design experiences that reward alignment over obedience. Make your brand so unapologetically itself that even shoplifting becomes brand storytelling.

CHAPTER 21

THE HIDDEN GENIUS OF GREEN M&MS AND SPELLING ERRORS

"To the untrained eye, it's chaos. To me, it's a system."

— MSV Doctrine, Article XXIII

CASE STUDY 3:

Go ahead—open your inbox and scroll through the digital dumpster fire known as your spam folder. You'll see the usual suspects: fake invoices, miracle supplements, and some shady prince who desperately needs your help moving money out of a volatile region. Personally, I get close to 1000 garbage messages a day. But there is one that should stand out to you. It's the one (or several) with a spelling error, a stretched-out logo, or a sentence that sounds like it was written by a confused AI on NyQuil.

Now pause and ask yourself: "Are you like Neo in *The Matrix,* effortlessly dodging digital bullets and spotting the BS as soon as it hits your periphery? Or are these scammers just bumbling overseas amateurs who can't mimic your region's dialect? Or...

...was that glaring spelling error *put there on purpose?*

The truth is unsettling: *most of the time, it's intentional.* Why? Because that "mistake" is actually a brilliantly evil filtering mechanism.

You see, scammers have no interest in arguing with the hyper-alert, detail-obsessed, grammar-correcting elite. Those people are too smart and will be a waste of time and resources. They don't want a debate; they want a fish that *bites the hook hard.*

Those spelling errors? They're not mistakes. They're *qualifiers.*

They're looking for the kind of prospect who doesn't notice red flags. Someone who sees a distorted bank logo and thinks, "Looks legit." It's pre-screening at scale. If you respond, you've already failed the test.

This is how you scam at scale.

Now let's take a look at how this villainous tactic has been used productively as opposed to destructively.

Remember Van Halen's infamous demand for a bowl of *only green M&Ms* backstage? At first glance, it looked like a band of spoiled rock divas demanding snack segregation. But it was actually a brilliant move, cooked up by their lawyer to serve as a hidden compliance test.

Van Halen's stage show was a towering monster of lights, pyrotechnics, and machinery. One wrong setup could literally kill someone. The green M&Ms weren't about ego, they were a canary in the coal mine.

If the band walked into a dressing room and saw red, brown or yellow candies mixed in, they knew instantly that the promoter hadn't read the full rider. If they missed the candy clause, they probably missed the important stuff, like rigging specs and safety protocols.

One errant red M&M? Boom. Mandatory safety check. Genius.

So what's the takeaway here?

Lesson:

You don't need to wait for a discovery call or a funnel click to qualify a prospect. Sometimes the smartest move is to design your own version of a misspelled phishing email, or a green M&M. A signal. A trap. A test.

Your Mission:

Want to know if your prospect reads thoroughly? Embed a bizarre but harmless line in the fine print of your proposal, e.g. "Please confirm your favorite dinosaur in your reply." No dinosaur? No deal.

Qualifying doesn't always have to be obvious. In fact, the best qualifiers are *unseen by all but the right kind of people.*

And those people? Those are your people.

CHAPTER 22

LET'S STEAL FROM A 7-ELEVEN

"I'm not a thief. I'm a collector of overlooked opportunities."

— MSV Doctrine, Article XIX

CASE STUDY 4

Tonight, we're not robbing Fort Knox. We're knocking over a 7-Eleven.

Not literally, of course. This is about brand heists. Taking what works, repackaging it with villain-level brilliance, and selling it back at a premium. Let's dissect how Joe C. Thompson stole from the entire grocery industry and created a global empire.

The Setup:

I once had a client panic on a call. "I sell milk! If Walmart moves in and sells it cheaper, I'm doomed!"

My reply: "You don't sell milk."

"Yes, I do," she said, getting defensive.

"No, you sell something completely different. Something you can't touch."

You see, in 1927, Joe C. Thompson, the manager of Southland Ice Company in Dallas, Texas, had an idea. He opened a tiny store that sold only staples like milk, eggs and bread. Not at the back of a sprawling supermarket, but right there, on the ice dock.

No parking lot obstacle course. No cart convoy through endless aisles. No waiting behind someone checking out 78 cans of creamed corn. Just grab, pay, and go.

And for this convenience, people paid more. Willingly.

This wasn't a discount store. It was a decommoditized experience.

Thus, the first convenience store was born.

The Price of Convenience

Fast forward to the late 1980s, Joe's humble little store is now an international franchise called 7-Eleven. There is a standup comedy boom, and every comic has a bit on the sticker shock of 7-Eleven prices. People mocked the idea of paying $4 for a soda, but they still paid for it. Why? Because speed, location and ease beat out saving 75 cents every time.

Then came the next evolution: delivery. DoorDash. Uber Eats. Postmates. The meme machine now targets $20 Big Mac deliveries with $9 in fees. And yet, people still hit "order."

Every layer of convenience adds a layer of cost. Until competitors catch up. Then you find the next layer. Rinse, steal, repeat.

What Can You Steal?

So what are you really selling? Is it milk? No, it's the illusion of saving time. Is it bread? No, it's the rush of instant gratification.

And it's that stolen valor you feel for some reason when you return home and your significant other says, "Wow, that was quick!"

Joe Thompson didn't invent bread or milk. He didn't rebrand eggs. He invented a process. A customer experience. They both culminated into a byproduct: a shortcut. And shortcuts are the currency of a distracted, busy society.

Lesson:

What is your industry's equivalent of a convenience store? What if you cut the process in half?

Up the premium. What are your customers paying with besides money? Time? Energy? Effort? Fix it.

Your Mission:

Combine thefts: Take from 7-Eleven, DoorDash, and Warby Parker if you must. Blend your heists into something new.

Innovation is just creative theft at scale.

Remember: steal from one person and you're a thief. Steal from a hundred? Now you're a genius.

Now go. And try not to leave fingerprints.

CHAPTER 23

THE SECRET SWORD STYLE OF EASTER EGG MARKETING

"Mastery isn't declared. It's discovered—hidden in the shadows of your strategy."

— MSV Doctrine, Article XXII: Sword & Signal

CASE STUDY 5

Every great supervillain needs a bit of swordsmanship. Not just to vanquish enemies, but to **defend our creative ideas**, sometimes at the tip of a metaphorical blade. After all, what is a pitch meeting if not a duel?

While I haven't yet *mastered* the blade, I've been studying. Today's dark art? The concept of **Oku Lai.**

In samurai culture, *Oku Lai* refers to **coveted, whisper-level techniques** in swordplay passed down only through word of mouth. No written records. No video tutorials. No 12-step infographics on LinkedIn. Just a lineage of trust. These hidden maneuvers were treasured not just for their effectiveness, but because **only the worthy ever got to learn them.**

These techniques weren't just about cutting power; they were about exclusivity. Possession of an *Oku Lai* technique wasn't just tactical, it was identity. A mark of inclusion. A declaration of: "I know something you don't."

Now ask yourself this: How can your brand create that same feeling?

How do you make your prospects feel like they're part of an inner circle? Like they've been handed a secret code that no one else is even aware exists?

You deploy the hidden blade of modern marketing:

Easter Egg Marketing.

An Easter egg is a concealed gem, a message, image, or feature hidden in your product, site, or brand experience. They're usually found in software, games, films—anything built by a team with **a twisted sense of humor and a god complex.** (The first easter egg was noted in the 1979 Atari 2600 video game Adventure, where savvy gamers could uncover the developers' name displayed onscreen if they knew the secret of how.)

If you've ever discovered one, you remember that *thrill*. You were told by a friend. Or you stumbled upon it. Either way, **you became one of the chosen.** The elite few who "got it."

The best part? You couldn't wait to **tell someone else**, but only if they were worthy. Sound like *Oku Lai* to you?

Exhibit A:

Type "do a barrel roll" into Google. The entire screen does a 360. Pure chaos. Zero explanation.

Exhibit B:

Activate Siri and whisper "LUMOS." Your iPhone's flashlight switches on. Cast a second spell: "NOX." It turns off.

You've just crossed into the realm of *Oku Lai*. But digitally. And virally.

And if the experience hits that **perfect mix of secret + cool**, something sinister and glorious happens:
Your audience *wants* to share it
... but only with those they deem worthy.

That, my fellow villain, is **power**. Not clicks. Not views. But *earned evangelism*.

You didn't shove your brand down someone's throat.
You handed them a secret. And they became your messenger.
Voluntarily.

So let me put this in our villainous vernacular:

Marketing is no longer about attention. It's about initiation.

Design a moment so hidden, so clever, so rewarding, that it becomes *ritual*.
Something they whisper about in Slack threads.
Something they show off like a tattoo they earned in battle.

And yes, I'd be a hypocrite if I didn't walk the walk.

So here's your first *Oku Lai* technique:
Go to **decommoditized.com** and **find the hidden Easter egg.**
(It's not that hard. But the unworthy will never notice it.)

Let's see if you're worthy.

CHAPTER 24

CONCLUSION

"The greatest crimes are the ones that feel like art."
— Unknown (but definitely someone cool)

If I were a betting man, I'd wager that if you've made it this far, you, like I, think in non-conformist ways.

I know this because...

You and I, we're not so different.

There's a quote that resonates deeply within my organization:

"Heroes see danger in the world and attack it head-on. Villains see the madness in the world for what it is and decide to shape it to suit their means."

We're designers, thought leaders, marketers, non-conformists. It's tempting to fight against the chaos, to swim against the tide, to "fix" what's broken. But let's face it, that's a recipe for burnout, disillusionment, and certain defeat. If you truly want to succeed in this game, you have to play by a new set of rules. Your rules.

Much like Captain Kirk and the Kobayashi Maru, in order to win, you need to rewrite the game.

That's what this life is about. Creativity isn't clean, efficient, or safe. It's messy, unpredictable, and a little dangerous. If you wanted to be safe, you'd have become an accountant. But that's not who you are. You've chosen this wild, treacherous path of creation, a career that's inherently unsafe.

And that's where the magic lives.

By definition, you, a creative, non-conforming, strategic marketing mastermind, are already levels above anyone else in their respective fields.

Who better to repackage and rewrite the rules of their industry than someone with your exact skill set?

Lean into this dangerous lifestyle you chose. Tap into the chaos and the possibilities. Use it to rewrite the rules of *your* game.

This is your tipping point, your defining moment. Will you continue to play it safe? Will you continue to sacrifice a tiny bit of yourself with every client who asks you to tap the depths of creativity for something "fresh, new and unseen" and then retreats into the safety of what they already know? I invite you to stretch farther, push harder, and challenge the boundaries of what's possible in this field of ours. This dangerous, exhilarating field where the odds aren't just stacked against you, they're actively trying to pull you under.

And let's not forget: when 85% of people are hardwired to resist change, it's far easier to make enemies than allies.

Woodrow Wilson said it best: "If you want to make enemies, try to change something."

So let's embrace it. Let's revel in the madness, the resistance, the chaos. I say, "Let's go out and make some enemies!"

Credits

Supervillainous Editor In Chief: Nick Ambrosino
Co-Editor: Thomas Chiesa
Cover Design: Brendan Bailey
Shout Out: Charles Leyte for showing me that Playstation commercial

Keep In Touch:

www.decommoditized.com
www.marketingforsupervillains.com
www.SPRVILLN.com

ABOUT THE AUTHOR

Jesse James Wroblewski has been orchestrating marketing mischief from his lair in New York for nearly three decades. His work is equal parts genius and madness and has been featured in *Rolling Stone, Fangoria,* and the book *505 Weirdest Websites Ever,* as well as countless media outlets that didn't know what hit them.

After decades inside an industry that rewards conformity and punishes originality, Jesse rebuilt his philosophy from the ground up. What emerged wasn't just a new direction; it was a new identity. The Marketing Supervillain™ was born, not out of rebellion, but out of necessity. *Marketing For Supervillains: Volume 1* was his villainous monologue, the "WHY" behind the madness. Volume 2 is the "HOW." An unfiltered blueprint for building your unfair marketing advantage and taking back control from the committee of the clueless. This isn't career advice. It's an invitation to join the revolution.